10 Powerful Strategies to Support Literacy Using Bilingual Books

10 estrategias poderosas para apoyar la alfabetización con libros bilingües

Valerie Butrón and Dr. Rita Guzmán

ISBN 9798218554019

These 10 strategies can help students develop proficiency in both languages, fostering biliteracy through engaging and thoughtful use of bilingual books.

Estas 10 estrategias pueden ayudar a los estudiantes a desarrollar el dominio de ambos idiomas, fomentando la alfabetización bilingüe mediante el uso atractivo y reflexivo de libros bilingües.

Researchers and teachers have found that bilingual books or dual language books provide serious advantages that motivate students to read for pleasure (Zhang & Webb, 2019).

"Bilingual books help children transfer conceptual knowledge and skills across languages, and compare and contrast concepts across languages, and therefore are effective at helping students develop vocabulary across languages" (Semmingson, Pole & Tommerdahl, 2015).

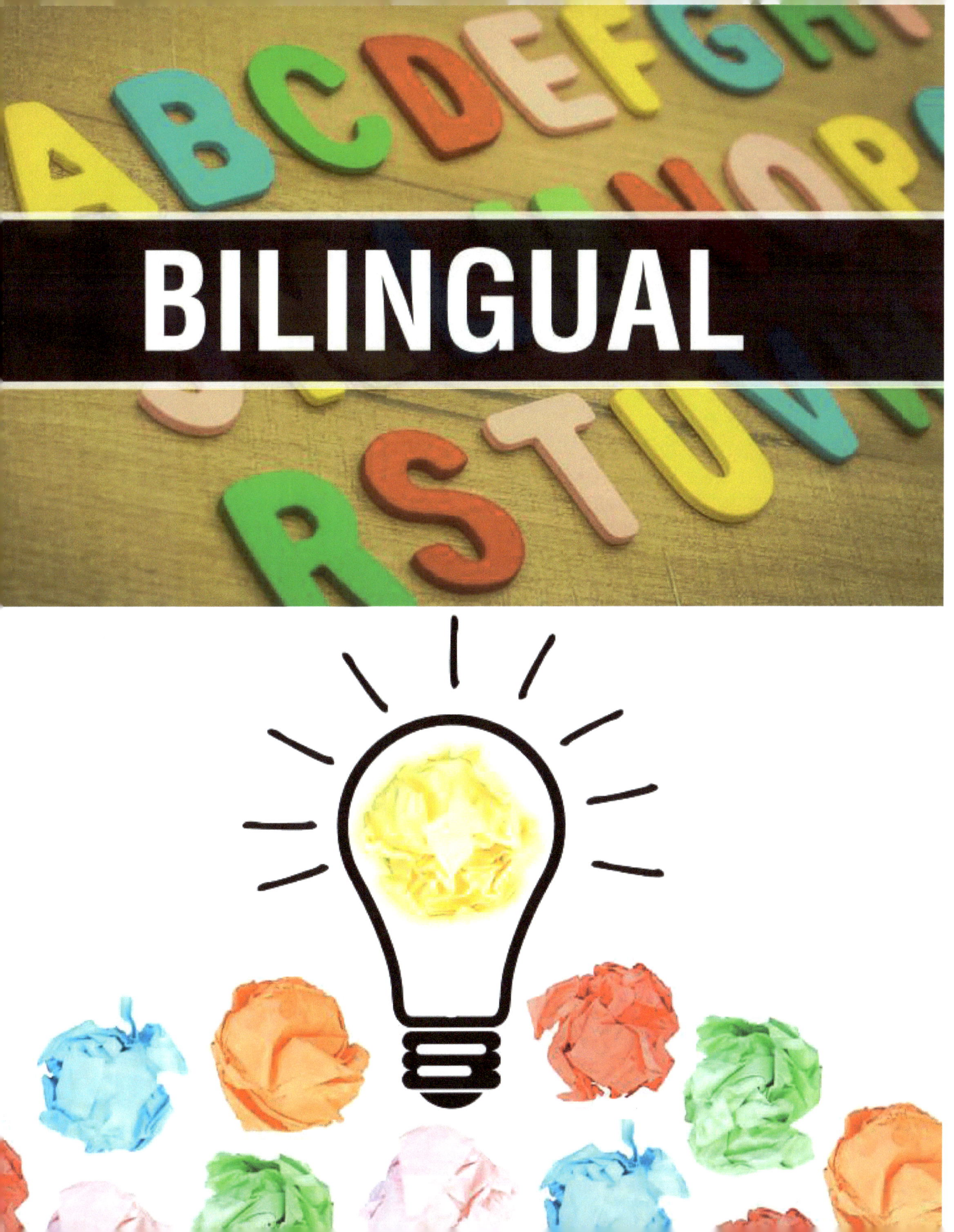
BILINGUAL

Read Aloud in Both Languages
Leer en voz alta en ambos idiomas

Alternate Reading: Read the same book aloud in both languages, alternating chapters or sections. This helps students understand the story in their stronger language while being exposed to the new language.

Lectura alternativa: Lea el mismo libro en voz alta en ambos idiomas, alternando capítulos o secciones. Esto ayuda a los estudiantes a comprender el cuento en su idioma más fuerte mientras están expuestos al nuevo idioma.

Model Fluency: Read with expression to demonstrate fluency and intonation in both languages, helping students grasp the nuances of each.

Modelar la fluidez: Lea con expresión para demostrar fluidez y entonación en ambos idiomas, ayudando a los estudiantes a comprender los matices de cada uno.

Encourage Side-by-Side Reading
Fomentar la lectura en paralelo

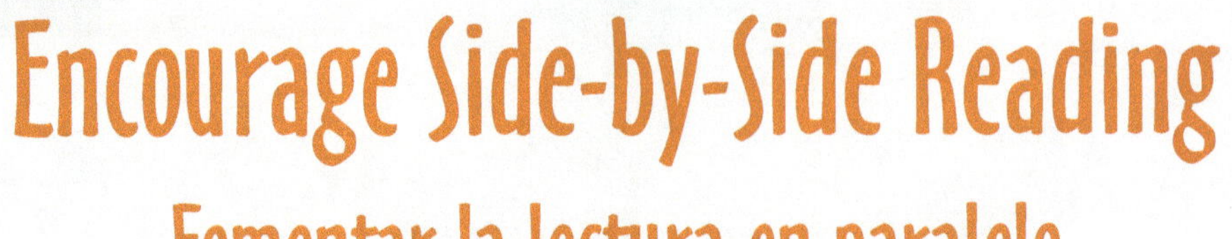

Parallel Texts: Use bilingual books where the text is presented side by side, in both languages. This allows students to see the direct connection between the two languages, increasing vocabulary recognition and comprehension.

Textos paralelos: Utilice libros bilingües donde el texto se presente uno al lado del otro, en ambos idiomas. Esto permite a los estudiantes ver la conexión directa entre los dos idiomas, aumentando el reconocimiento y la comprensión del vocabulario.

Self-Checking: Students can self-check their understanding by referring to the translation as they read.

Autoevaluación: Los estudiantes pueden autoevaluar su comprensión consultando la traducción mientras leen.

10 Powerful Strategies to Support Literacy
Using Bilingual Books

3

Use Books for Vocabulary Development
Utilice libros para el desarrollo del vocabulario

Pre-Reading Vocabulary: Before reading, introduce key vocabulary in both languages. Have students identify and track these words throughout the text, making connections between the two languages.
Vocabulario previo a la lectura: Antes de leer, presenta el vocabulario clave en ambos idiomas. Hace que los estudiantes identifiquen y sigan estas palabras a lo largo del texto, estableciendo conexiones entre los dos idiomas.

Word Walls: Create bilingual word walls that highlight key terms from the books. Students can refer to these walls when writing or discussing the text.
Muros de palabras: Crear muros de palabras bilingües que resalten los términos clave de los libros. Los estudiantes pueden consultar estos muros cuando escriben o discuten el texto.

4

Engage in Cross-Language Discussions
Participar en discusiones en ambos idiomas

Multilingual Discussions: Facilitate group discussions where students can respond to the text in either language. Encourage them to translate parts of the conversation to ensure understanding across languages.

Discusiones multilingües: Facilita discusiones grupales donde los estudiantes pueden responder al texto en cualquier idioma. Anímalos a traducir partes de la conversación para garantizar la comprensión en todos los idiomas.

Compare and Contrast: Ask students to compare how certain phrases or ideas are expressed in both languages. This deepens their understanding of language structure and usage.

Comparar y contrastar: Pida a los estudiantes que comparen cómo se expresan ciertas frases o ideas en ambos idiomas. Esto profundiza su comprensión de la estructura y el uso del lenguaje.

10 Powerful Strategies to Support Literacy Using Bilingual Books

5

Writing Activities in Both Languages
Actividades de escritura en ambos idiomas

Bilingual Journals: Have students maintain bilingual reading journals, where they reflect on the story or its themes in both languages. They can switch languages for different entries to practice writing in both.

Diarios bilingües: Haga que los estudiantes mantengan diarios de lectura bilingües, donde reflexionen sobre la historia o sus temas en ambos idiomas. Pueden cambiar de idioma para diferentes entradas para practicar la escritura en ambos.

Translate and Adapt (6th-12th grade): Assign translation exercises where students translate short passages from the book into the other language. They can also rewrite parts of the story with their own twist in either language.

Traducir y adaptar (grados 6.º a 12.º): Asigne ejercicios de traducción en los que los estudiantes traduzcan pasajes breves del libro al otro idioma. También pueden reescribir partes de la historia con su propio giro en cualquier idioma.

6

Highlight Cultural Contexts
Resaltar los contextos culturales

Cultural Discussions: Many bilingual books focus on cultural themes. Use the content to discuss the cultural contexts presented in both languages. This promotes not only biliteracy but also bicultural understanding.

Discusiones culturales: Muchos libros bilingües se centran en temas culturales. Utilice el contenido para discutir los contextos culturales presentados en ambos idiomas. Esto promueve no sólo la alfabetización bilingüe sino también la comprensión bicultural.

Relating to Personal Experiences: Encourage students to relate the cultural content of the books to their own experiences, using both languages to express their thoughts.

Relacionarse con experiencias personales: Anime a los estudiantes a relacionar el contenido cultural de los libros con sus propias experiencias, utilizando ambos idiomas para expresar sus pensamientos.

7

Pair Students for Collaborative Reading
Emparejar estudiantes para lectura colaborativa

Language Partners: Pair students with different language strengths to read bilingual books together. One student may be stronger in one language and help the other navigate unfamiliar vocabulary or grammar.

Compañeros lingüísticos: Combine a estudiantes con diferentes dominios lingüísticos para que lean libros bilingües juntos. Un estudiante puede ser más fuerte en un idioma y ayudar al otro a navegar en vocabulario o gramática desconocida.

Peer-to-Peer Teaching: Let students take turns reading aloud in each language and explaining the text to their partner, promoting peer learning.

Enseñanza entre pares: Permite que los estudiantes se turnen para leer en voz alta en cada idioma y explicar el texto a su compañero, promoviendo el aprendizaje entre pares.

8

Use Bilingual Books for Independent Reading
Utilice libros bilingües para la lectura independiente

Leveled Bilingual Books: Provide students with bilingual books that match their reading level in both languages. This supports independent reading and allows them to strengthen their weaker language at their own pace.

Libros bilingües nivelados: Proporcione a los estudiantes libros bilingües que coincidan con su nivel de lectura en ambos idiomas. Esto apoya la lectura independiente y les permite fortalecer su lenguaje más débil a su propio ritmo.

Track Progress: Have students record what they read in both languages, noting any new words or phrases learned. This helps build confidence as they see their skills develop.

Seguimiento del progreso: Haga que los estudiantes registren lo que leen en ambos idiomas y anoten las palabras o frases nuevas aprendidas. Esto ayuda a generar confianza a medida que ven cómo se desarrollan sus habilidades.

10 Powerful Strategies to Support Literacy
Using Bilingual Books

9

Interactive Activities
Actividades interactivas

Bilingual Book Clubs: Create bilingual book clubs where students can discuss the book in both languages. Incorporate activities like role-playing scenes in both languages to reinforce language skills.

Clubes de lectura bilingües: Crea clubes de lectura bilingües donde los estudiantes puedan discutir el libro en ambos idiomas. Incorpore actividades como escenas de juegos de roles en ambos idiomas para reforzar las habilidades lingüísticas.

Interactive Read-Alouds: Use read-aloud sessions to ask comprehension questions in one language and have students respond in the other. This encourages them to switch languages fluidly.

Lectura interactiva en voz alta: Utilice sesiones de lectura en voz alta para hacer preguntas de comprensión en un idioma y hacer que los estudiantes respondan en el otro. Esto les anima a cambiar de idioma con fluidez.

10 Powerful Strategies to Support Literacy
Using Bilingual Books

10

Leverage Technology
Aprovechar la tecnología

Digital Bilingual Books: Use digital platforms that provide bilingual texts with features like audio narration in both languages. This can help students with pronunciation and reinforce listening skills in both languages.

Libros digitales bilingües: Utilice plataformas digitales que proporcionan textos bilingües con funciones como narración de audio en ambos idiomas. Esto puede ayudar a los estudiantes con la pronunciación y reforzar las habilidades auditivas en ambos idiomas.

Language Apps: Incorporate language-learning apps that offer bilingual book activities, helping students practice vocabulary, grammar, and comprehension interactively.

Aplicaciones de idiomas: Incorpore aplicaciones de aprendizaje de idiomas que ofrezcan actividades de libros bilingües, ayudando a los estudiantes a practicar vocabulario, gramática y comprensión de forma interactiva.

References

Colorín Colorado. (n.d.). A bilingual site for educators and families of English language learners. Retrieved from https://www.colorincolorado.org

International Children's Digital Library. (n.d.). Free digital library of international children's books. Retrieved from http://www.childrenslibrary.org

Semmingson, Peggy & Pole, Kathryn & Tommerdahl, Jodi. (2015). Using bilingual books to enhance literacy around the world. European Scientific Journal.

Šifrar Kalan, M., Muñoz-Basols, J., Robles-García, P., Strawbridge, T., & Sánchez-Gutiérrez, C. (2024). The impact of multilingualism and proficiency on L2 vocabulary knowledge: contrasting high and low multilinguals. International Journal of Multilingualism, 1–24.

Zhang, Zhiying & Webb, Stuart. (2019). The effects of reading bilingual books on vocabulary learning. Reading in a Foreign Language, 109-139.

Dr. Rita Guzmán,
author & co-founder

Valerie Butrón,
author & co-founder